BLUE GUIDE

PHOENIX **POETS**

BLUE GUIDE

STEPHEN YENSER

THE UNIVERSITY OF CHICAGO PRESS
Chicago and London

STEPHEN YENSER is professor of English and director of the creative writing
program at the University of California, Los Angeles. He is the author of three
critical works, and the coeditor of the collected works of James Merrill. Yenser's first
book of poems, *The Fire in All Things* (1992), won the Walt Whitman Award of the
Academy of American Poets.

The University of Chicago Press, Chicago 60637
The University of Chicago Press, Ltd., London
© 2006 by The University of Chicago
All rights reserved. Published 2006
Printed in the United States of America

15 14 13 12 11 10 09 08 07 06   1 2 3 4 5

ISBN: 0-226-95134-0 (cloth)
ISBN: 0-226-95135-9 (paper)

Yenser, Stephen.
  Blue guide / Stephen Yenser.
     p. cm. — (Phoenix poets)
  ISBN 0-226-95134-0 (cloth : alk. paper) — ISBN 0-226-95135-9 (pbk. : alk. paper)
  I. Title. II. Series.
  PS3575.E53B59 2006
  811'.54—dc22

                                                        2005023011

To Melissa and Helen

bhel-[1]. To shine, flash, burn; shining white and various bright colors; fire. **I. 1.** Germanic*bala-*, white mark in Old English *baellede*, bald (<"having a white head"): BALD. **2.** Celtic *belo-*, bright, in *belo-te(p)ina*, "brightfire," name of a prehistoric spring festival (*te[p]ina*, fire; see **tep-**): BELTANE. **3.** Russian *byelii*, white: BELUGA. **4.** Greek *phalaros*, "having a white spot"; PHALAROPE. **II. 1.** Suffixed variant form *bhle-wo* in Germanic *blewaz*, blue, in Common Romance *blavus*: BLUE. **2.** Suffixed o-grade form *bhlō-wo-* in Latin *flāvus*, golden or reddish yellow: FLAVESCENT, FLAVIN, FLAVONE, FLAVOPROTEIN. **III.** Various extended Germanic forms. **1.** *blaikjan*, to make white, in Old English *blǣcan*, to bleach: BLEACH. **2.** *blaikaz*, shining, white: BLEAK 1; **b.** Old Norse *bleikja*, white color: BLEAK 2. **3.** *blas-*, shining, white, in: **a.** *blaese*, torch, bright fire: BLAZE 1; **b.** Middle Low German *bles*, white spot: BLAZE 2; **c.** Middle Dutch *bles*, white spot: BLESBOK; **d.** Old French *blesmir*, to make pale: BLEMISH. **4.** *blend-*, *bland-*, to shine, blind, dazzle, confuse, in **a.** Old English *blind*, blind: BLIND (BLINDFOLD), (PURBLIND); **b.** Old High German, to blind, deceive: BLENDE; **c.** Old Norse *blanda*, to mingle: BLEND; **d.** Old French *blond*, blond: BLOND. **5.** *blenk-*, *blank-*, to dazzle, shine, blind, in **a.** Old English *blencan*, to decieve: BLENCH 1; **b.** Middle Dutch *blinken*, to glitter: BLINK; **c.** Vulgar Latin *blancus*, white: BLANCH, (BLANK), (BLANKET), (BLANC-MANGE). **6.** *blisk-*, to shine, burn, in Old English *blyscan*, to glow red: BLUSH. **IV.** Variant forms *bhleg-*, *behlg-*, to shine, flash, burn. **1.** Germanic *blakaz*, burned, in Old English *blaec*, black: BLACK. **2.** Germanic *blikatjan* in Old High German *blëcchazzen*, to flash, lighten: BLITZKRIEG. **3.** Zero-grade form *bhlg-* in: **a.** Latin *fulgere*, to flash, shine: FULGENT, FULGOR, FULGURATE, EFFULGENT, FOUDRAYANT, REFULGENT; **b.** Latin *fulmen* (< *fulg-men*), lightning, thunderbolt: FULMINATE. **4. a.** Latin *flagare*, to blaze: FLAGRANT, CONFLAGRATION, DEFLAGRATE; **b.** Latin *flamma*, (*flag-ma*), a flame: FLAME, FLAMBEAU, FLAMBOYANT, FLAMINGO, FLAMMABLE, INFLAME. **5.** Greek *phlegein*, to burn: PHLEGM, (PHLEGMATIC), PHLEGETHON. **6.** Greek *phlox*, a flame, also a wallflower: PHLOGISTON, PHLOGOPITE, PHLOX. [Pok. 1. *bhel-* 118, *bheleg-* 124, *bhleu-(k)-* 159.]

"Appendix," *The American Heritage Dictionary,* ed. Calvert Watkins

Contents

IV

V

VI

Acknowledgments

The works listed below originally appeared, sometimes in different versions, in the following publications:

Another Language of Flowers: Paintings, Dorothea Tanning with poems by
    various hands (George Braziller): "Loveknot *(Flagrantis*
    speculum veneris)"
The Antioch Review: "Salle Archaïque: An Afterbeat." Copyright © 1994 by the
    Antioch Review, Inc. First appeared in the *Antioch Review*, Vol. 52,
    No. 1. Reprinted by permission of the Editors.
The Colorado Review: "To Fall" and "Ghazal: Of Names"
The Michigan Quarterly Review: "Tidepools: La Jolla" and
    "*Spirare*: Evening at Point Dume"
The Paris Review, issues 129 and 167: "Blue Guide," "Polo Lounge,"
    "Numbers" (as "Jazz Spot"), "Shutters"
The Partisan Review: "Kerouacky"
Poetry, May 1996: "Los Angeles Fractals" (as "A Day in the Life")
Prose Poems at Work, 2001: "Lunaria" (as "Stepps")
Smartish Pace: "Valedictions" and "MRI: A Trance"
The Southwest Review, Vol. 89, No.1, 2004: "Sfakian Variations"
The Yale Review: "Paradise Cove," "Harmonie du Soir," and "Inkles, Shreds
    & Scales"

*

"After Cavafy" (in "Valedictions") also appeared in *All about Doris: A Portfolio.*

"Blue Guide" also appeared in *Best American Poems 1995*, ed. Richard Howard and David Lehman.

"Paradise Cove" also appeared in *Pushcart Prize XXV*, ed. Bill Henderson.

"Ghazal: Of Names" also appeared in *Ravishing Disunities: Real Ghazals in English*, ed. Agha Shahid Ali.

"Kerouacky" also appeared in *Sixty Years of American Poetry (Expanded Edition)*, ed. Bruno Navasky.

"Harmonie du Soir" also appeared in *Poetry Daily: 366 Poems from the World's Most Popular Website,* ed. Diane Boller, Don Selby, and Chryss Yost; and in *Poetry Calendar 2005,* ed. Shafiq Naz.

I

Loveknot (Flagrantis speculum veneris)

Dorothea Tanning's painting

I am flesh and flower
That each other devour.
Tongue-tied lovers know
It's myself I swallow.

MRI: A Trance

For my daughter

So there I am at Tower Imaging
(*Imaging . . .* Yes, yes: I'm aging!),
Drugged against the claustrophobia—
O heart, O troubled heart—a live shell
Of myself, levered into the bridal
Chamber at last, so to speak.
And I have left my metal—
My watch and coins, my pen, my keys,
My belt and zippered slacks—and donned a gown
And though scared stiff been slid condemned
As a condomed
Phallus into a pulsing place,
Where I lie listening through earphones
To KKJZ-FM,
Playing just then the Bill Holman Quintet
Playing "Out of This World."

*

Under the broadcast music, another's din:
Percussive, pneumatic, Dionysian,
Pounding in and out and in in some
Code of its own, in some remorseless Morse,
The pictures of my favorite feelings' quarters.
We're looking at the plumbing, the PVC,
And something called the Bundle of Hiss.

We're eavesdropping on the heart's tick-talk,
Enthusiastic tachycardia.

I don't know how to phrase this synaesthetic cling.
It's not at all clear what is happening,
Or when. We're loading every riff with ore,
Maybe. Or waiting to explode. Or maybe make
A broken consort's music of these fears.

*

Now, as foretold, we go through several "phases—
Or movements." Although *I* am motionless.
Sedately terrified. My life aflow
Behind closed eyes, I flatly fail
Not to remember all these years ago,
So long before you squeezed into our world,
Crawling the passageway to Cheops' penetralia
To find—nothing. A lidless sarcophagus,
Emptier than a skull's eyeholes.

*

During the break between the Five That Thrive
And Sweets and Trane, I hear cicadas,
An eerie ostinato
Making the breezy music of a Cretan olive
Tickle the ear, until I pick up your great-grandpa's
Blowhumming through his tissue-covered comb,
As we drive by neat rows of winter wheat back home.
And off in that past's future I make out
The lonesome cricket who sits in, jams in,
One evening in the Sunset Canyon Center

In Westwood, California,
So thrilled to find his finely calibrated
Kind so finely celebrated,
As William Merwin reads his poem called "Black Jewel."

And now I hear some ice cubes, all whiskeyed up,
Tinkling under Erroll Garner's right hand—
Or is it my father's, as he sits listening
To "Blue Lou" and "Misty" on a 78,
Smoke unfurling from the other hand's brown Raleigh,
And waiting for that last high note, pure as a tuning fork's.

*

Or say that one right now, right there, could pluck
A single string of a Cycladic harp
In front of the Temple of Athena Nike,
Itself harplike by moonlight
That night of the eclipse,
When all around me calcined marble and bedrock,
Polished by centuries of pilgrims' soles,
Slippery as ice, black and white as tramped-
through snow refrozen years back in Wisconsin,
Shone up from underfoot
Back at the moon, its maria like smog-eaten pits
On a tumbled drum that Earth's dark swallowed
As it must (*The Emerald Tablet*: "As above,
So below") minute by minute. Minute

By minute now the tranquillizer ebbs,
And to my aging, still sublunar ear the tone
Finally struck is just a smidgin sharp.

It pricks this bubble, although another one
Will one day lift and lovely drift me off

(With all the trances, travels, and travails
That, leaving you, I've imagined leaving you,
Ravels and ravelings, recordings,
The broken string
Of my rebab, my *suk* Arabic, my taxi Greek
Somehow restrung to sound in scheme and skein
Notes that float across the bars)

Like something you chased yesterday across the lawn . . .
Today is not that day, and so they pull me out.

Spirare: *Evening At Point Dume*

Its origin's unknowable,
But since in it one spirit leaves yet cleaves
Unto another, perhaps the Proto-Indo-European,
Itself perhaps a kind of verbal smoke ring
Uttered with a glottal stop,
Meant *ghost* and *breath* at once.

Then it would be as though we were to find
"Aphorism" and "horizon" rhizomatous,
Sprung from some Ur-word meaning *definition*,
And in the process to eliminate
Limits between
The flatly said and flatly seen
And to illuminate by its black light
Impossible conversations,
As of sea and sky,
In a kind of pastel spindrift or sfumato.

As though to see how "diligence" bled into "elegance."
As though to say "precocious" ripened merrily to "apricot"
And deliquesced to "drupe,"
Or "stranger" once implied both *host* and *guest*
(The former's home a *hostile hostel*
Providing bread and fruit and rest)
And rhymed with "ghost."
As though to think that *reddish, ashen,* and *blue-black*

All lived in "livid," one whole sunset
And perfect plum of a word.

As though, dear Helen, there were a surd,
A tiny slice of P-I-E
That meant indistinguishably
To shine, to flash, to burn
And in its flaming out, the shedding of its light,
Limned "bleak" and "blaze" alike,
And "blond" and "blink" and "blind"—
Though never, ever "bland"—
As well as "blank" and "black" and "blue" between.

Or a flower to offer you: "Ghost's breath."
Almost a spirea, like meadowsweet,
Or hardhack, or bridal wreath.
Almost an otherworldly flower.
Aphrodite's, say. Maybe Persephone's.
Not, dear God, Eurydice's.

Paradise Cove

My daughter in the coastal sunset asks for Plato. "Plato,"
She begs, "*blue* Plato, please, *Plato*" . . . Finally, I understand

And rummage from the picnic basket the Play-Doh, the blue can,
And the pink as well—which henceforth I call "Aristotle."

"Ariso'l, Ariso'l," she repeats—then, swallowing the glottal,
"Aerosol," and there we are, playing with both ideas that there are.

For one, this mixogamous world is all one thing, and for the other,
This waxing unicity is always two (or more, which is the same,

Since to rub two things together in a ruttish realm is to get others,
And those yet others, viz. our daughters and their sons).

The temporizing third idea—that these two are somehow one—
Returns us to the first. So Marcus Aurelius thought. Maybe Lao Tzu.

In any event, Nietzsche teaches that each thinker's goal and due
Is to become as serious as a child at play, even as the sun sinks,

Even when again the sun is setting—or rather, here in Los Angeles,
City of Angels, City of Angles, the set is sunning—stunning,

Even, in ever acuter, gentler rays that with the smaze
Turn the horizon Technicolor pinks and blues, lavenders and zincs.

Helen's Zen

Today you told us how a too-tight shoe
Gave you such a headache in the foot.
In your next breath you said you'd made a wish.
I said, Why don't you wait till it comes true,
So that it *will*, and tell it then? You said,
You didn't think that you could *do* that. Why not?
Because I wished that we would die together,
You and Mommy and me, and when we're dead—
I don't think that we *talk*. Well, I said—
As for your foot . . . By then you'd gone ahead,
I think that maybe only souls go *through*,
You know? You know, I said, you say "You know"
Too much? Anyway, the soul, you said,
I hope it has a belly button, don't you?

"*Harmonie du Soir*"

Hampton's last concert in Santa Monica

That ever younger evening sky's pastel accord's
A chord off Santa Monica
Even now, deepening shades of spent
Shadings, jazzy, night jasmine's pungent
Fadings in up from Virgin's blue
Through hues as interfused as tones in a harmonica
To cobalt blue, to coalfire blue, to Coltrane blue,
Smoky and chuffing, to blooming lavender of jacaranda
Flowers that fail, that fall across lanai, gazebo, and veranda,
Those years before your birth.

A Santa Ana blew . . .
The stars came out . . . kept coming out . . .
Above the dimming earth . . .
On stage . . . *For as above, so here below* . . .

In "The 'Original' Stardust" the vibraphone solo:
As cocky as cocaine with each angelic line
Struck off in its constellation,
And then snuffed out, as fine as that cocaine
They used to stanch the pain
Before they broke my nose that time to fix

My broken nose, melody racing out in front, looping around
The orchestra—balletic, teasing, like a fox—
Until it's clear that it could go
On forever and so starts

Stopping, begins to
Skip like a heart, or to limp
Like Mother Killdeer in disguise,
To double-hitch down to a kind of foxtrot,
Hunted, haunted, caught,
Danced with by the whole libidinous band
An endless moment, then abandoned,
As it must be, like Valéry's pure poem,
A little lion, or unicorn, until the phallic horn
Flares up like sunset,
Ever so sweetly, compliantly, discreetly,
Each gold or gilded gliding sound well worth its silent wait,
To blow the by then barely, still
Hardly flaming foxbreath out.

There, now: play it at the wake,
From flashes to ashes, from dusk to dust,
As though in time with sacring bell and censer swinging—
"Les sons et les parfums tournent dans l'air du soir,"
Dans le beau de l'air du soir . . .
That's how I want to leave you when I must.

Tidepools: La Jolla

Quick, mystic—this is the world's profoundest mirror.
The girl in any of us leans a little nearer.

You lean to it this evening, Helen Emily,
Holding my hand, to glimpse us both, though dreamily,

As like your breath that fogs my morning shaving glass
It dries up seaward, leaving sea moss, black tape grass,

Scary weeds—also a puckered seam of seaspray,
A pinch of which you put your lips to, then spin away—

Barefoot, braid swinging—from a broken breaker, your shrieks
Bringing a cloud wisp's blush-brushed color to your cheeks,

Then kneel again to moons and trumpets, scallops, dollars,
And mermaid fans and purses, anemones and tiny stars.

Another winter day, my love, when you are older,
That is, when we're both older (half-bolder and half-colder),

Maybe you'll walk back down here to this place—
If whose precise location trafficky years erase

From memory, no matter, since to it the sun
Blazes a narrow path each cloudless day that's done—

And see how I could come once more to recognize
This world's whole hoard one evening in your filling eyes.

II

Sfakian Variations

Postcards to JM

A goat's bell wakes us—he's in a tamarisk!—
as the cicadas translate
with their vibratos early light's moiré
shimmerings rebounding from the bay
into our high room's whitewashed plaster.

So that's the news to ruminate at breakfast.
No politicians abolishing disaster,
no strings attached. Or *à la* Mallarmé,
it's all pure music—physics, that is to say—
and everything is strings that vibrate.

*

Melba toast, fresh orange juice, and coffee.

A *horiatikí saláta*, bread, and beer.

Ouzo with three ice cubes and appetizers
and then a plate of "local fish" for dinner.

And in the interims I read Cavafy,
Stevens, and Yeats and worry that I hike
too much just in my head through stubborn stonebrash
herbs and common shrubs, dry and spiny,
to swim in precious shallows—turquoise, sapphire.

*

This is a country for old men. Cicadas
in Judas trees, and bumblebees among
the bougainvillaea, succulents, a few
native goldfinches in their cages hung
above taverna tables. The beach is stony,
the "ruins" hardly qualify, each trek
sounds too austerely beautiful to take.
And one might see from one's own balcony,
which has the peaks as well as bay in view,
a lammergeyer swoop to an old goat's carcass.

*

God gave out gifts to Crete: to Kissámos,
wine heady as kisses; to Ierápetra, olives
fleshy and sharp; dark cherries to Amári.
When the swaggering Sfakiots at last appeared,
their daggers gleaming, only rocks remained.
—And how have you provided for *our* lives,
they asked him.—Use your scrubby brains, God sneered.
Can't you see those farmers work for you?

*

Beside our table on the littoral,
as we're about to close the books this evening,
the hill again stands pat, and the sun
folds again, and the server folds
our parasol, and water laps the rocks
louder, begins to come into its own,
a mood—a mode—that concentrates, that rocks

the rocks awake to darker, colder colors,
preparing to be serious, no longer
marginal. To take us literally as breaths.
We have to change our lives? We have to die.

*

Here in one poem, just "a few lines"
(*olígous stíchous*), sixteen to be precise,
anyone can find the crucial terms,
several proscribed in English verse
today, and in the order quoted now.
"Tasteful" (*kalaísthyton*) and "polished" (*leíon*),
constelled around the name of one Ammónis,
they include "subtle beauty" (*leptí emorphiá*),
"elegant" and "musical" (*oraía* and *mousiká*),
and prove the "craftsmanship" (*mastoriá*)
of Constantine Cavafy and inextricably
his "grief" (*lipí*) and "love" (*agápi*)
and everywhere his "feeling" (*aísthima*)
"for our life" (*apó tín zoí más*),
especially for one man, dead long before,
exemplary poet and Alexandrian.

*

Mornings, a trance of cicadas,
invisible, incessant.
A weave of dense white noise,
except it's really a translucent,
gauzy green, the vibrant color
water is near the shore at noon.
An intense tinnitus,

and like that last a hint to us,
perhaps, of the sound eternity is—
the great susurrus of silence
avant la lettre, so to speak.
Though it's here all the time.
Usually we just don't notice.
We hear it too in the inaudible
voices, the traces of voices
that we have heard and read.
It's not after all as though they're not us.
Cavafy says they come to us
then fade like music at night.
Another way to put it is
that we fade into those who note us.
We ventriloquize each other,
perhaps. Although your ashes
are half this world away, my friend,
if you are anywhere, you're here.
Sometimes you just don't notice.

*

Evening's tavernal transactions make one think
that so much happens in between. It's *in*
between, I mean. On CD Lady Day
moans "Them that's got shall get,
them that's not shall lose" and thus calls up
Cavafy's masterly refusal, whose point
I took from a loved book you gave to me
decades ago. What I didn't take,
I cannot say, as someone must have said.
Cavafy said that to decline is to
decline thenceforth, and I'm inclined, today,

to agree. Yet there are negatives
that we take confidently to our graves.

*

This could be paradise. Because one does not want
to leave? *Except* one does not want to leave?

Why, Zeus himself preferred to be interred here,
as he was born here in an inland cave.

But somewhere my airplane's on schedule.
These days, these words, both fall so quickly into place

I think I'll fall myself as Icarus
fell right out there because he couldn't wait

before I've made known what it is I do want.

*

Mín ksináchte, you inscribed my book:
"Don't forget." A short but long Greek sentence.
Don't lose the thread, Daedalus told
Ariadne to tell Theseus. And yet,
how not to do so, not even he could say,
and his precocious Icarus forgot.
When Theseus abandoned Ariadne,
ripe, faithful, sleeping on the shore,
the gods forgot him, so he forgot
to change his sails from black to white,
and so his anguished father died, misled.
Never losing himself the thread,

Daedalus solved the tiny labyrinth
of a triton shell. As I think Pound,
himself imprisoned by his own creation,
might have remembered outside Pisa
("an ant's forefoot shall save you").
Mín ksináchte. And yet how not?
The knotted phrase goes on through its own maze.
I leave its book to my daughter, whose name is Helen.

*

Soon it will be the right time.
The resident kitten, so affectionate
at first blush, will turn out to be
neurotically needy. The proprietors'
adorable infant son will smile
too little to be truly endearing.
The plumbing, the mosquitoes, the seamier
undersides of the local nightlife . . .

Time to dispose, dispense, pack up, reflect.
Despair at how to take back all one would.
Put things in order so the cleaning woman
won't recall one badly, should one return.
Write those few thank-you notes.
There's nothing else, really, to do,
at last. The sunscreen, the local maps,
a guide book or two, the ferry schedule—
one can leave them behind for now, for others.

*

Goats bawl and goats' bells clink
and ice in the glass of ouzo tinkles back
and that is all the music—even *tzitzíkes*
rest and listen—anyone needs
to face tonight, until the fog
settles in, thick and muggy, though cold
and clammy on the painted railing
around the balcony that overlooks
this whole small world one nearly overlooked
and now can't bear to leave
where the taverna lights grow dimmer
by the minute now and then are hard
to make out as a dwelt-on memory
and then and now are gone.

III

Salle Archaïque: An Afterbeat

Then toward the end she showed him the Apollo,
So he could weigh what he'd said Rilke said . . .
"We can't conceive of his appalling head
In which eye-apples ripen. But his torso
Still glows out like a gas-lit streetlamp's globes,
Wherein his gaze, only turned down low,

Holds its own and burns. That pectoral swerve
Otherwise couldn't blind you, and that wry
Twist of his marble thighs could never light
Up with its smile the very source of birth.
Otherwise this stone would stand disfigured
Under the shoulders' broad, still lambent curve,

And would not shimmer like some predator's pelt—
Or break out from its compass like a star.
It has no facet that does not regard,
Indeed see through you. You must change your life."
The next month, trailing her pen down what he'd felt
He felt, she smiled—and changed his "life" to "wife."

Ghazal: Of Names

For DA

Today, my friend, when all the scarified world implies a web,
This *ghazal* is for you, who told me that word signifies a web.

When Stein saw in a lightning strike "the difference is spreading,"
Her insight lit up all the acts from which arise the web.

Your Tigris's meandering cursive's far from my rap city's.
And yet beneath each culture's rhapsodies there lies a web.

You know, because he was a weaver too, that Webster knew,
Because all languages are foreign, they must comprise a web.

Cow pat, *Kuhhandel*, cow's parsley, *la voie lactée*—it's all a mesh.
Scrutinize the wings: each dung-drawn, web-doomed fly's a web.

From their own pincerlike, pararachnid vantages,
Egoists like Saddam and Bush presume to tyrannize the web.

My friend, whose name, suppressed perforce, can mean *physician*,
Vesalius showed how selfhood will just disguise the web.

Ghazali, self-exiled like you from Baghdad, sought certitude.
He found the Cosmic Soul that unifies the web.

Now here I am, giddy in Yiddish, dizzy with *ghazal*-dazzle,
Arch fornicator, satisfied he ramifies the web.

Los Angeles Fractals

Along the main drag in South Central this is what one sees.
As in so much of this mazed congeries, or these
Cities, or rather multiplicities,
In this noncity of ethnicities,
El Pueblo de Nuestra Señora la Reina de los Angeles de Porciúncula,
Where *SRO* means poverty, not popularity,
This absolutely *loco* new world *Logos*
Breaking in all directions like a snooker rack,
What one sees rolling by is signs. Signs and ads, marquees, logos,
Billboards, and flapping posters overlapping
Or pasted flatly next to others, as in Bearden's street scenes
(In his words, "Throwing, say, *violet* against *orange*"—
As though to say *violent* against *syringe*,
As though to plunge the needle deep into the fruit,
Maybe to the tune of a creaking *doorhinge*,
If the butler in the emerging murder plot has got a Cockney accent),
And brand-new ads and flyers on ads and emblems sheared
Off, others emended by graffitists, or worn sheer,
Exposing ghosts of older signs,
The names and mottoes weathered into—palimpsests? pentimenti?
Signage: signs of age in our Age of Signs.
Or into something like the glazes, scrapes, and stencils
In Larry Rivers' cool and jazzy canvas,
The one that shocked me in the shabby lobby of Manhattan's Chelsea
So many loopy years ago on my way to Iraq from Kansas.

Looking at the map, trying to find a route to The White Horse,
I saw how each point points at last to every other point and course . . .

ABC Market   Connection Motel—Welcome Day Sleeper   SACRED HOLY
GHOST TEMPLE   Guaranteed Used Tires   Orchid Corsages and Funer signs
SMART AND FINAL IRIS   American Iron Nipple Mfg. Inc

Close to the Chelsea, in The White Horse, Dylan Thomas drowned
His catawampous brain and its whole litter of new rhymes
Just two years after Einstein died.
Einstein's brain meanwhile was pickled, packed off to Wichita,
About the time that Bearden gave up writing songs and saw
That "Collage is the art form for our times"
And started slapping blacks and blues on sunny hues,
And Davis stoked John Coltrane into his own "Kind of Blue"
Which chugs and chugs today for miles and miles.
About the time my father first got fired.

("Fired up," in his rendition.)

The old man in my trial, in South Gate, charged with DUI,
Kept reminding me of father,
Except this man was black, with indigo tattoos,
And with convictions just as visible, and with shin sores
Like bitten chocolate-covered cherries
The Public Defender had him hike his cuffs to show,
Arlechino luckless, old, and slow,
And self-effacing, and "poor as dirt"
(As my grandfather liked to say, really *liked* to say,
Who'd worked for the federal land bank and who'd know).
But *au fond* he was just a charming lush.
The City argued that, although no one was hurt,
He'd scraped a parked car with his Pinto—and then run.
Open and shut, the City said, like his car door.

One night in Wichita, bicycling to "the corner,"
My father veered into the curb and pitched like an Apache
From a mustang shot broadside in black and white in "Fort Apache"
(Which featured its own dipsomaniac,
Downtown at last that summer at the Orpheum,
Our finest family theater, on a double bill with "Baghdad")
Across the flawless, chromed, and sexy wings
Of my best friend's new three-speed Monarch.
My father broke two teeth and bloodied his already muddied speech.
Numbed, stunned, forlorn as Orpheus himself,
For once he came back home without his fifth, unstrung.
My friend could not forgive him for the bending of a wheel.
Part Cherokee like him—indeed, like Bearden—
I could not forgive my friend.
                    And so I'd hold out for acquittal.

Vine Baptist Church El ino Allegre Melos Machine Tool Rebuil Chique Travel
Agency Angel's Assamblers Used Store Luis Uposteri Eros Towing

My father loved to waltz, across the living room, right knee aplant,
At twirls, intricate, hard, between my mother's thighs—
Or my girlfriend's. He had played starting guard for Friends,
And then played contract bridge, then poker, snooker . . .
Sang in The Singing Quakers and in a barbershop quartet (KFBI's),
At picnics crooned *"Volare"* and "Ol' Man River,"
Crosby crossed with Old Crow,
A blend of corn and wry, schmaltz and proto-scat,
Blacked his face with burnt cork for the vaudeville's minstrel show,
Smoked Raleighs for the coupons
The colors of tobacco stains on his right hand
(And of the streaks on underpants he later would not change),
And browned and blacked and shrank his lungs,
Stuffed the drum table's drawer with bills—unpaid—

And played it like a drum
On evenings Andy turned up with his alto sax to jam,
To jam and toast the major angels,
Jack Daniel, Paul Desmond, and Jim Beam, and beam and beam,
Years before the beams would turn to moonshine, then white lightning.

After decades playing buyer for Beech Aircraft
And then the spare part in an old friend's new machine shop,
He saw in a flash one looming Sunday on the riverbank
That he was meant to own a billiard parlor,
With tables too for checkers, pitch, and dominoes.
But then he got laid off his "interim job" in sporting goods
And spent his last unaided weekends catching carp with bloody dough.
"Bloody dough"—still not a scavenger himself,
Still literate, not yet mosquito-bit,
(If it was not booze-caused encephalopathy, if meningitis
Was not my canny mother's shady doctor's term for the insurance
        form),
Not yet an inmate of St. Francis' Second South
Among the other isolates dramatically beside themselves,
Each deep in private conversation, dueling and drooling,
Behind the steel doors grilled and barred and locked—
He'd have sneered at the British pun: "bloody dough."

Evenings, with the streetlights, he'd get lit, and sigh, or drone
"I only want to be as good a father as my own,"
Or chant "Get a little drunk and you land in jail . . . "
If Mother was still up to hear,
He might break into "Abdullah Bulbul Amir."
In his last job he tried to sell things on the telephone.
"You have a velvet voice," his youthful, busty, truthful boss observed.
Because he'd had a stroke by then, and things were simplified,
In that he took real pride. Then had a seizure. After he died,

Among the bills that crammed the secretary,
I found a postcard, unstamped, preaddressed to a local mortuary—
Filled out in part in a child's printing scattered with tipsy caps—
Requesting information on how to "Reduce the High Cost of Dying."

CHURCH'S FRIED CHIC*** *LosТAngeles Tool & Die Church of the City of
the Angels South LosТAngelesТBody Shop Tool & Die Buy One Dawn's Early
Bite SAMMYS BILLIARDS—Free Cues*

Those spray-painted *T's*—for the South Gate "Trays"?
Although he'd lived on "the frontier,"
The ever-, never-changing ghetto's stiletto edge,
Always newly nicked and always sharply honed,
Where "tool and die" would mean—translated—*carpe diem*,
He was still a deep-dyed racist.
"Well, let me think on *that*," he'd scowl and hedge,
But mean, "So let me drink to *that*,"
And make his way outside "to water."

He never used our nozzle, just his big, brown thumb
Across the threaded fitting to shoot or flatten,
To spray or arch the stream.
He'd blast the driveway clean of vagrant oak leaves
And blow the lazy drifts of spider webs out of our arbor vitae.
More Pennsylvania Dutch than Cherokee,
He scoured and scoured and scoured the porch
And shot the dead Dutch elm leaves off the lawn, over the curb,
Into the gutter, down the street.
A connoisseur of evanescence, Riverside's Heraclitus—
Riverside's *Rivers*, it strikes me now—
He stood and fanned the water out to conjure rainbows,
And roped the water into diamond ovals,
Our "Poet Lariat," and then with quick, cursive loops

Calligraphed it into script we couldn't follow.
His signature in water, say, or lyrics that he had by heart—
"Tired of livin' but scared of dyin'"
(Which one night at a party came out "Tired of dyin' but scared of
    livin'"),
Or "If I were Huckleberry Finn, what trouble I'd be in . . . "
He loved word games and awful rhymes.
He'd quote the backside of that business card
He carried in his wallet ("Genuine Cowhide" in gilt)
Whose cryptic lines were half at least of what I thought was poetry:

> —Seville, der dago,
> A towsin busses, innaro.
> —Napoli, dems trux,
> Summit cows in, summit dux.

I think now that he might have been—well,
All alone, and thinking, drinking, linking
(*What are you thinkin', Lincoln?*),
And making of it all what he'd make too when he would nod
Beside the Little Arkansas, his creel beside him, and his fishing rod,
His boughten jar of dough or Folgers can of dug night crawlers.
He would have thought my mother up, their fight the night before,
When she yanked out a clump of his black hair.
He would have thought his father up from under close-mown sod,
Who'd worked security on White House grounds—
Which was why we had the sap and the baseball signed "Babe Ruth"
(Which Mother later gave to my brother's friends for batting
        practice)
My father kept inside the unlocked strongbox,
With the scuffed-up leather-bound insurance sheaf,

And the hexagonal cufflinks with diamond chips.
The sap—the sap was magical, its sweat-tanned leather pungent with its
    power.
So when a boy got stabbed,
I asked if I could take the sap to school.

*The Rose Mot** LIZ'S LOUNGE Erose Massages FATHERS OFFICE Mecca
Motel SMART AND FINAL Complet Detail Janes Residential Care Service
Bays Open Please Come In*

City of angles, saxes, jukes. Of singles, sex, and jewels.
Of the Lost and Jealous. The Angelless. L/Aliens.
Shangri-L.A. El Lay Grande. The LA-byrinth, sick of tryin',
With centers everywhere, like Pascal's God, in plazas and pavilions,
Minimalls for drive-bys, drive-ups, minimaulings,
Carjackings, gangbangings, gaudy private compounds . . .
"Uh-huh, this is Lozengeless," as my polyglot,
My exiled, suave, intensely hoarse Iraqi friend observes.
What are the limits of its mesh and mess?
As these States to the world at large, so L.A. to these States?
The concrete universal! On hypothesis,
The many things the world is
Are at bottom one thing
"Circling the drain,"
In the LAPD's colorful stock phrase.
But there's no end to synecdoche.
The coming "casino park," LA'S VEGAS,
Features a Disneyland with its own replica of Legoland's Manhattan.
City of sights. Sea city. Cecity.
The slipknot keeps on tightening around the shrinking neck.
In front of me, there in that tightest of our later native forms,

The license plate, I found advice, both frank and wry:

SIGNIFY.

I'd seen a Wichita State decal on one of the *nafarat* in Jumhuriyah
     Square.
The first time that I'd seen a movie set for real was there
As well. In Mesopotamia.

"Between two rivers."

Like "Wichita."

Going to court, I drove along the long
Pseudo-Assyrian façade of Samson Tyre & Rubber, so-called when it was
    built,
And now The Citadel, a supermall, its 1920s bas-reliefs (restored)
Of wingèd genii copied from the palace at dar-Sharrukin.
Omne, with a basket in his left hand, a pinecone in his right,
Repeated his part near Babylon in some dark rite
Whose special expiations still elude us.

Waiting for a light,

I gave in to the other jurors, angry, nervous, penurious, and certain,
Who'd better things to do than sit around and think
About the obscure origins of lustrous words like *guilt*.

The sun, earning its setting, stopped, just behind our palm,
Its indenting fronds, late that afternoon in Baghdad
(Los Angeles of the Middle East!—
But with a single traffic light
And roundabouts everywhere, cars weaving lane to lane),
Cradling the fire opal above a skyline vaporizing,
This new war we've begun ('04) materializing . . .
And now the dry *click-clack* of dominoes
And tric-trac float back up through neon curves
Of Arabic and lights festooned throughout cafés
Below my balcony that overlooked the Tigris

At 105 D/1 Abu Nawas
(Named for the bibulous poet and venerist
And parodist of holy desert verse),
Where I sat with my *arak*, clearer than the tapwater.
Swallows and pigeons flew in and out of parching shade and trees,
And when they hit the sunlight looked like spinning coins
As their wings winked.
                    Heads or tails?
                        My father
Would wink and flip to see who got to break the rack.
Now and then a pigeon tried to climb a steep, steep gust,
Bellying up, flapping, clapping sillily for itself,
And then slipped over, headfirst, as on a waterslide—
Or, having given up at last on the *au-déla*,
Slid back down.
                "Train on a grade, out of fuel . . . "
                                Tails or heads?

Cottonwood leaves were dark then wet with sunlight in the breeze
Where we lay on the bank of the Little Arkansas,
Tam and I, afloat on sloe gin and the radio's black jazz,
Trying to turn our futures into silky stories.
How could such tales be spun,
And how could spinning heads be asked to make much sense of them,
If not in mental sheers and in air pockets such as those

(LAX NEXT RIGHT . . . Next: LAX LAST EXIT . . .
Here's to lacks. Desires. Connecting flights . . .)

Such as *these*, I mean, above the balconies
Above the Tigris, itself (in Thoreau's resurrection) "extra-vagant,"
As it just keeps on rolling along.

Above, volitionless as flotsam, swallows hang
In azure air. In thick blue air. "*Nel blu, dipinto di blu*," my father
      sang.
Dipinto di blu: and we dip into the blue,
Once more, the blue no sooner blew than blown—
No sooner shut than open, in this seismicity,
This fugacity where anything that flies has by now flown.
The swallows' wings—*Volare*—dip
Like quills, or no, like brushes into blue
They brush a deeper shade, as evening blushes, sinks
In like ink, like thinking,
Gradual as this evening's drinks, sinks in and swallows
The swallows, flown like time into itself.

So here's to Time, whose sentences we serve concurrently,
Whose syntax we pay out like line when due,
Whose accidents—*fallings on* and in and out—we have.
Or don't. Like children. And here's to Guilt,
Glimmerings dimming out anew,
Like lightning bugs whose inner lights we squeezed,
Sherry and I, into letters binding us
Forever across our knuckles in the graveyard by the tracks,
Rolling stock rocking, shocking by—
Stockcars, boxcars, flatcars, tankers, hopper cars—
Carrying cattle, weapons, fuel, fruit, the homeless,
And all we'll want into the future where we are.

IV

Valedictions

Charles Gullans (1929–1993)

We pass,
Hélas:
Ci-gît
C. G.,
Whose life
Penned strife
And passion
Fashioned
From rough-
cut stuff,
Deep-mined
As diamond,
Verses
Terse,
Faceted,
Tacit.

Joseph Riddel (1931–1992)

His machine lied
And didn't the day he died:
"Hello. Riddel here.
Or rather, *not* here.
Who's there?
Where?"
Old roll-out quarterback
Deconstructs the sack.

Doris Curran (1932–2000)

After Cavafy, "Che fece . . . il gran rifiuto"

Some of us cannot avoid the day
when we must make a clean decision: No or Yes.
It's always clear at once who's ready to profess
a Yes that's ripe within, and once he's had his say,

he's swept along on principles and cheers.
She who resisted, meanwhile, wouldn't change her mind.
If she'd been asked again, again she'd have declined,
though No—the *right* No—hobble her her remaining years.

Lorna Roberts (1942–2001)

After Rilke, Die Sonette en Orpheus, II.12

So choose to change. Be inspired by Fire,
where something hides whose transformations stun.
Author of all that's earthly, that drafting spirit
adores each burning figure's turning point.

What wills itself *to stay* has fossilized.
Can it believe it's truly safe in stone?
Listen: from far away, Hardness itself
summons the hard, as it lifts its hammer.

Knowledge knows well who wells up like a freshet
and whom to lead beside creation's waters
where sources often end and ends spring up.

Every blessèd space they stroll through, awed,
derives directly from Departure. And Daphne,
leaving in laurel, wants you to be the wind.

Robert Lowell (1917–1977)

After Montale, "Il ramarro, se scocca"

The green lizard, if it streaks
through stubble
in the stifling heat—

the sail, when it whips
and dips from the shock
of the rocks—

the noon cannon
weaker than your heartbeat
and the chronometer if it
soundlessly springs—

. . . .

and then? In vain the lightning
flash changes you to something
rich and strange. It was different, your die.

To Fall

Where are the songs of spring?

And what of summer's own cadenzas   *Verb sap*   They've also gone
Quick   Oh quick   as the slaughter of camellias on the lawn

and other little accidents   soft as laughter   soft as collisions
in *kaleidoscope*   say   shards reflowered a moment in the mirrors

Or take that fire obscurely kindled back in spring's *feuillage*
as in my German surname   obscene in Yiddish   she took for years

Take the resonance as deep as resin in   say   *liquidambars*
Take coals banked in their leaves   November's embers' burs

massed above as in a test for color blindness   the sun
just squinting through   Or take our blindness   our head-on collusions

And now time's fullness   epitomized in apricots
In pits of apricots   In pits like words   Each word a stone

Kerouacky

I want my Partotooty
Sweetie backpie back
                   — *Mexico City Blues*

But now where are those lovely, early fogs,
Those sheer, cheery, cherry smogs
That jazzed up the evening sun
Before it went out for orgasmic nights
In crazy organzas of blushes and jacaranda blues?

In the old days, the bold, the bop days on the beach,
In the starry daze of those fried nights, those satyr days,
Skinny-dipping, cocky, nippled in the bud,
Hip and slaphappy, dripping moon and copping feels,
They promised that they'd leave no tern unstoned.

Riffs, they wanted, rough drafts, *the gists and piths of poesy,*
The jism, just drift and spin—and lowest tides got high with them,
Before they roach-clipped the kick-sticks and, bushwhacked, lipstuck,
Hellbent, slabhappy now, laid some rubber, split
To crash, and to record some slipsticked Zs.

They never cried over spilt milk, spilt pot, spilt seed,
Back before the tarring of the feathery tribes
(So to speak), the greasing of palms, the rigging of the bay . . .
One night someone changed the sign to read:
"$50 FINE FOR LETTERING."

Back before that, we were still learning
How to treat in turn the nasty sewage badly,
And the city's sordes of insults rolled off the coast
Like water off a great merganser's back . . .
One morning it was all thick crude.

So here's one more, one long, one wasted breath,
No doubt, axed out of that beat, beat, beat past
To weave into a blasted wreath
To float out over those wraiths, bested but blessed,
Oiled, maybe, but still *smooth*, *baby*, and *gone* at last.

Across the Bar

Jumbo's Clown Room

No, no—please have a seat. Right here. God knows this prosaic situation needs
a muse. So why not help me down a couplet, nip a bud or two. We might
even—to adapt the coinage of one of our clerical poets—sip at a couple of neat
niplets. Well, coinages. But whether all that glitters should be guilt or not, it's
sure a bush in hand is worth two birds in Britain, no? Oh, don't go yet. The
other day I saw this woman's eyes in the rear view mirror of her Lexus talking
clearly as though she wore a veil. They drew me up beside her. I watched her
rouge her lips, then kiss them, urge the lighter back into its socket, then mouth

her radio's malady—a blues, I'd guess, the way her shadowed eyes meaned down. The sting of her mascaraed lashes. Like yours. Her cheekbones, polished, made one squint: want naught, waist naught. And think before you cry. No moaning here. Keep your liner, wit, and powder dry.

Polo Lounge

So one day the late Bird highly fortified strolls into this posh *boite* itself and down there, leaning on the bar, is Wallace Stevens (newly arrived, old LL.D. tucked away, sheepskin in wolf, flirting with the minishirted bartendress), whom he welcomes. My friend, a hard man's good to find, as we used to say over in The Styx. Here it's an altogether different fettle of quiche, of course. It's still the early word that gets the berm, the latter *pater* patters back and hunches over. Hey, my alto ego, does that point have a story? the other asks, and orders up—with Lady Day's delayed demise in mind—a stiff White Cadillac. In the beginning was the Weird, one raises his glass and stipulates, and then the other, Be thou me, Bops, and then the Lucid and the Ludic juke on off, a pair of irrational numbers, each trying to hang longer, surds of a certain weather, simply patriarchal, Old Testicle and New together.

Lunaria

Was jazz baroque then? A music broken then? Or a sort of bankrupt consort, for those immusical as we, hanging out off the numbingly circled square of rock 'n' roll in the darkly ruinous, urinous alleys and strips whose screechy, oily, smoke-belch seductions we couldn't squelch in those rubber-burnt, jet-fueled years to come. How all that clamor glamored us from Grandma's grammar right through pot to chamber music (to Bartòk by way of bartalk, Ginsberg, and the well-initialed DT's language's gauged gouges, complete with background honks, and sticks run down the bars of early Cages, to Satie by way of satiation with Joplin's jalopies, solos on straight pipes, and chops on one-holed flutes) and thence to opera was something that we'd one day have no time at last to figure for ourself.

Shutters

Sunset and evening star and yet once more the "Gymnopédies"? Who shuffled
our deck of seedy CD's so lackadaisically, if you please? But here, take my man
Tambo, who liked an ale with serious hops (although he'd seen a friend pur-
sued by spirits through St. Vincent's ER right to the abyss). On the one hand
his disciples did not know what meter was. On the other hand they did not
know a thing about God, let alone the Lamb and his twelve steps and how to
parlay-voo erection into deposition and another coming, although one seemed
to remember he had been guided by a pompous pilot. But on the third hand
there was nothing in between they knew. *Iamb that iamb*, he yelled one day and
leapt. They looked sheepish back—witnesses say—and did not jump.

Numbers

Nice piece, n'est-ce pas? So having sheared
A hydrant and a high wire pole you hit a tree,
You say, with three
Friends, and snapped a femur

Like stemware. Water skied.
Downed lines sparked and danced.
You were not fried.
But ambulanced.

Barreling upstate on Route 20
Scott LaFaro stopped at his
Tree instantly
Too and at 30

Died. You were 19
That year your two
Friends died and one
Did time for it

And amphetamines.
Little purple hearts.
These days they get 70
Radio stations here.

Some are vintage jazz
You were not at the wheel
Humming with at 90
But could have been as

You blasted home to get
The sawed-off shot-
gun you had got
Just for that bouncer—then chopped

The hydrant off.
                    If one could play
His cards the way
Bill Evans plays his
Yamaha that Sunday matinee

Two weeks before LaFaro crashes,
Because LaFaro plucks
His bass as colorfully
As a Dutch pheasant

While Paul Motian brashes
Zen measures on rice paper
Drumheads, if time could stay
A still life flowing with its oils

Like that, then one could know,
You say, that he was dead
Forever and it would be o-
fucking-plucking-kay.

Variations on Ovid

For JKY

Vivit et armiferae cornix invisa Minervae (Amores II.6)

Like Mother's screaming,
the crow's caws seem to rip its
own bloody throat out.

*

Father's Old Crow hid
in our garage till you smashed
dead its dad-gum head.

*

Each dawn's hangover,
the cock sang his own crowbar
or two, poor bastard.

*

Next year a tire iron
meted out to my bombed skull
seventeen stitches.

*

Scorched angel fallen
to pine's tip, Christmas's crow must
cope with mad songbirds.

*

Craving blackbird pie,
Astrid sought out books on rooks
and dug up *Macbeth*.

*

But though the raven
counts as crow, the blackbird's still
a quick thrush, craven.

*

When the dyer's hand
rolled two cold and coal-black eyes,
was the crows' die cast?

*

Because *C* was *K*,
"crow" is "work" backward. Back word,
black word: be caws, claws.

*

The adhamant clause,
clinging to one's every word,
vouches *This one counts*.

*

At the roads' crossing,
three crows pick at a squirrel
who would not eat crow.

*

The poets' host raised
a dark toast: may the best dressed
guest roast y'all in turn.

*

A loud, white fact here,
a cockatoo cries his crew
of crows through Bel-Air.

*

Black whole, the mind's eye's
pupil, takes bright teachers in,
straight as the crow flies.

v

Inkles, Shreds & Scales

"Always a knit of identity, always distinction, always a breed of life."
Walt Whitman, "Song of Myself"

Not a knot of identity, *nota bene*, though perhaps a net, a nanonet, certainly never a naught, a nit, the salt and whit of difference, the bread of life. The bread, the breed, the braid.

The bread of life. The stuff of life. The stiff stuff, if baguette or challah—the staff, the stave, the stanza. "Stanza my stone," as Stevens has it—who doesn't bother to specify—who skips—alchemy's philosopher's stone.

Because we cannot live by bread alone, however spelt. Or unless truly spelt. "Thy word is all, if we could spell" (George Herbert).

Language and food: mete them on the tongue. In the packing company cooler, I impaled tongues on hooks. I ground my teeth and thought of them as well-hung tongues. I called up Paul from Sunday school and tried to conjure "spiritual meat."

We get our daily "bread" from *bhreu-²*, to boil (*The American Heritage Dictionary*). Hence also "brew." And "breath." The primordial "broth." The bread, the brew, the breath. And "burn" (to heat, to brand, to fire) and "burn" (spring, stream, brook). The fire in all things. Burn, bourn, bourne—though not Hamlet's bourne, which would be a boundary.

"Not a knot"? But to be or not to be etc. Maybe one reason for this soliloquy's talismanic quotability is the pale fun of its veiled pun? The "not" makes a "knot": the Gordian question. At the heart of the matter. (The heart: a muscular organ. An organ: a work and an instrument.) The knot of the matter. Being, not being, being naught. The brood of life.

#

"*Text* means *Tissue*: but whereas hitherto we have always taken this tissue as a product, a ready-made veil, behind which lies, more or less hidden, meaning (truth), we are now emphasizing, in the tissue, the generative idea that the text is made, is worked out in a perpetual interweaving; lost in tissue—this texture—the subject unmakes himself, like a spider dissolving in the constructive secretions of its web. Were we fond of neologisms, we might define the theory of the text as an hyphology (*hyphos* is the tissue and the spider's web.)"
    Roland Barthes, *The Pleasures of the Text* (trans. Richard Howard)

"In other words, if Barthes had been less fond of neologisms, and a feminist, he might have named his theory of text production an 'arachnology.' . . . Arachne, the spider artist, began as a woman weaver of texts. By arachnology, then, I mean a critical positioning which reads *against* the weave of indifferentiation to discover the embodiment in writing of a gendered subjectivity."
    Nancy K. Miller, "Arachnologies: The Woman, the Text, and the Critic"

"Only as woman ('those who enjoy the use of the signifier [. . .], those who are comforted by their entrance into the language which constitutes for them a place of jouissance and of speech')—can men write."
    Alice Jardine, quoting and contextualizing Edmond Jabès
    in her *Gynesis*

Writing is gendered? Why not? Rilke thought so: "The deepest experience of the creative artist is feminine."

And yet that "entrance into the language" comports as well with the figure shaped by one of Rilke's translators: "The artist is a lover, and he must woo his medium until she opens to him; until the richness in her rises to the surface like a blush. Could we adore one another the way the poet adores his words or the painter his colors . . . "

William Gass, "The Artist and Society"

So in still other words, there are two things or forces or principles rather than one. The principle of two things itself implies a third thing—opposition or resistance. Or is that the one aboriginal thing? But then that one thing entails like an amphisbaena two? "There is one story and one story only." Over and over.

"It will be seen that there was an essential opposition between two aspects of Aristotle's influence . . . There are not many differences in mental habit more significant than that between the habit of thinking in discrete, well-defined class-concepts and that of thinking in terms of continuity, of infinitely delicate shadings-off."

A. O. Lovejoy, *The Great Chain of Being*

And yet "take any concrete finite thing and try to hold it fast. You cannot, for so held, it proves not to be concrete at all, but an arbitrary extract or abstract which you have made from the remainder of empirical reality. The rest of things invades and overflows both it and you together . . . In the end nothing less than the whole of everything can be the truth of anything at all."

William James, *A Pluralistic Universe*

Somewhere here there's an axiom to grind. Double-edged. Double-headed. Like a labrys. Like *labrys* and *labyrinth*. A single Carian root, a Greek *rhizoma*, a Knossian knot—a knot in the thread that is the route, as though the thread were the maze. (Penelope Reed Doob, *The Idea of the Labyrinth*: a maze is singly double, artistry and chaos, depending on one's point of view. Ditto Omar

Calabrese, *Neo-Baroque*: a labyrinth has "two intellectual features: the pleasure of becoming lost when confronted by its inextricability [followed by fear] and the taste for solving something.")

"The difference is spreading," in a word. (Gertrude Stein's.)

#

"Nature knits up her kinds in a network, not in a chain; but men can follow only by chains because their language can't handle several things at once."
    Albrecht von Haller, quoted by Howard Nemerov

Now that's a gage to engage. Doesn't even a lyric poem aspire to be a micro-ecosystem? If a poem, then a stanza—a word, if understood like a tree. Like the word *tree* steadfastly ramifying into *truth*. E-literature latensifies the branchy roots of things.

"[Things or in other words] complex adaptive systems—ant colonies, networks of neurons, the immune system, the Internet, and the global economy, to name a few—where the behavior of the whole is much more complex than the behavior of the parts."
    John H. Holland, *Emergence: From Chaos to Order*

E-literature: *elite rature*. Irresistible. As Robert Coover has it, "the allure of the blank spaces of these fabulous networks, these green-limned gardens of forking paths, to narrative artists [who may thereby] replace logic with character or metaphor, say, scholarship with collage and verbal wit, and turn the story loose in a space where whatever is possible is necessary."
    Robert Coover, quoted by George P. Landow, *Hypertext*

But to go back to brass tacks and trailing filaments:

> "The spider's touch, how exquisitely fine!
> Feels at each thread, and lives along the line."
>
> Pope, "Essay on Man"

From *lino-*, *linum* like a distaff (*stebh-*, *stephein*) spins out linen, flax, fibre, thread; string, sequence, row; *ligne*, *vers*, line. The thread of life, the bread of life, and the fine line.

Between prose
poetry's
the line &
crossing it's
another fine
wine—a lark,
a lurk to hark.

> "Outside, along the matted eaves, painstakingly, sweetly, wasps go over and over a honeysuckle vine.
> "Inside, the bellows creak. Nate does wonders with both hands; with one hand. The attendant horse stamps his foot and nods his head as if agreeing to a peace treaty."
>
> Elizabeth Bishop, "In the Village"

Painstakingly, sweetly, from Bishop's child's point of view. Or wasps and honey. Over and over. Outside and inside knit. Netted. Never neat. Both hands, one hand—each one a wand. Stamps and nods. Sweetstakingly. Swaps. Sweep-stakingly. Nods and stamps. The knit of identity. To be "painstaking" is to be pains-taking, but it's also to be pain-staking. One might stake a pain in the way that one stakes a bet. And if you're Bishop, the way one stakes a young tree or a vine—or a line. In any case, one can't but feel the aching in "painstaking." The net and very note of identity.

Id entity? "Children often assign several meanings to the same entity . . . . It is this plastic notion of essence that accounts for the tremendous popularity of toys such as the multiform 'transformer' as well as for the wide appeal of Play-Doh" (Eviatar Zerubavel, *The Fine Line*). Not to mention that of Heraclitus.

"rhapsody: L. *rhapsodia*, from Gk. *rhapsodia*, from *rhapsoidos*, weaver of songs, rhapsodist: *rhaptein*, to string or stitch together (see *wer-* in Appendix [base of various Indo-European roots; to turn, to bend] + *oide*. Ode, song (see *wed-*[2] in Appendix [to speak])."

"Appendix," *The American Heritage Dictionary*, ed. Calvert Watkins

#

"*teks-*: To weave; also to fabricate, especially with an ax; also to make wicker or wattle fabric for (mud-covered) house walls. (Oldest form **teks-*.) 1. TEXT, TISSUE; CONTEXT, PRETEXT, from Latin *texere*, to weave, fabricate. 2. Suffixed form **teks-la-*. a. TILLER 2, TOIL 2, from Latin *tela*, web, net, warp of a fabric, also weaver's beam (to which the warp threads are tied); b. SUBTLE, from Latin *subtilis*, thin, fine, precise, subtle (<**sub-tela*, 'thread passing under the warp,' the finest thread; *sub*, under; see **upo**). 3. Suffixed form **teks-on-*, weaver, maker of wattle for house walls, builder (possibly contaminated with **teks-tor*, builder). TECTONIC; ARCHITECT, from Greek *tekton*, carpenter, builder. 4. Suffixed form **teks-na-*, craft (of weaving or fabricating). TECHNICAL, POLYTECHNIC, TECHNOLOGY, from Greek *tekhne*, art, craft, skill. 5a. DACHSHUND, from Old High German *dahs*, badger; b. DASSIE, from Middle Dutch *das*, badger. Both a and b from Germanic **thahsuz*, badger, possibly from this root ('the animal that builds,' referring to its burrowing skill) but more likely borrowed from the same pre-Indo-European source as the Celtic totemic name **Tazgo-* (as in Gaulish *Tazgo-*, Gaelic *Tadhg*), originally 'badger.'"

"Appendix," *The American Heritage Dictionary*, ed. Calvert Watkins

In other words, the letter of Hermes become the spirit of Vertumnus become the law of Ovid is there in the very air entering the house through the gaps between the words or symbols in every written fragment, ragment, and Janus-faced or Thoth-headed dogma in drag. Over and over. In the alpha-bet, in what is laid down from those earliest tongue-wedges of language on, in the languishes and the long wages, the tongue sandwiches, and in the chit[chat]ab[ul(ul)ation] of any community, anything is potentially anything else. Thus "money," as Reb Wallace the book-wallah said, his steaming chi and chibouk going up in smoke, "money is a kind of poetry."

"Mysteriously enough, poor Miss Gurley—I know she is poor—gives me a five-cent piece. She leans over and drops it in the pocket of the red-and-white dress that she has made herself. It is very, very shiny. King George's beard is like a little silver flame. Because they look like herring- or maybe salmon-scales, five-cent pieces are called 'fish-scales.' One heard of people's rings being found inside fish, or their long-lost jack-knives. What if one could scrape a salmon and find a little picture of King George on every scale?

"I put my five-cent piece in my mouth for greater safety on the way home, and swallow it. Months later, as far as I know, it is still in me, transmuting all its precious metal into my growing teeth and hair."
Bishop, "In the Village"

Five cents: five senses: the quintessence of alchemy and crux: inner metamorphosis: outer transformation. The answer is "the problem is / how / to keep shape & flow," in Ammons's rhyme. As in the case of vision, in Oliver Sacks's hypothesis: "Whatever the mechanism, the fusing of discrete visual frames or snapshots is a prerequisite for continuity, for a flowing, mobile consciousness."

#

A rose in the word's a rose. Eros arose as roses. Roses are Eros's arrows. Arrows of the compass rose.

Well, so what? a faithful reader writes. This is all at best jokes and at worst lit crit. Clit Writ, he could have said. And there's a grin of truth in that. He gives good lip. All too trifling, too precious, and in short too *too*. Balletic babytalk. Or laptop dancing. As though *work* and *orgy* came together, as they did indeed in the beginning. In the Word, double-tonguing the labrysax. Getting the contrapuntal pun. Or the cuntrapontal, as my student wrote, or cuntrapetal, though we mustn't say so, unless we're feminine or intimate with wrinkles, inkles, culls. Ullage all. Inkles and threads, lingles and shreds.

Or: while Eros is not a ruse, he don't mean a thing if he ain't gotta sing.

Ach, my reader says: he continues a riddle while a Roma continues to burn. Word-weary, we must have walls in museums, zoos in cities, and in their places there the zebras, which must have no relations with D bras, which must shift for themselves. Divide, Divide! Separate and elevate. Keep it clean. And screw contact between.

"The linguals and labials among letters are particularly troublesome."
William A. Hammond, *Diseases of the Nervous System*

Our boulevardiers' favorite leading-edge magazine flatly will "not accept science fiction, erotica, westerns, horror, romance, or children's stories."

So "shall we tremble before clothwebs and cobwebs, whether woven in Arkwright looms, or by the silent Arachnes that weave unrestingly in our imagination?" So Carlyle, in *Sartor Resartus*, shuttling among Arkwright and ark-wright, ark and arc, Noah and Arachne.

Or shall we tremble *with* them, since in Brian Greene's summation "the theory suggests that the microscopic landscape is suffused with tiny strings whose vibrational patterns orchestrate the evolution of the cosmos" (*The Elegant Universe*).

Elegant like *diligent*: from *leg-*[1]: to collect; with derivatives meaning "to speak."

Again, if Richard Feynman's right, if "nature uses only the longest threads to weave her patterns, so each small piece of her fabric reveals the organization of the whole tapestry," then any gram of grammar might signify, any gaud be rejoiced in. The point would be the whole implicit in it. The sabulous bit of truth would be *yek-*, *to speak*, so to speak, around which a pearl accretes in which *joke* modulates to *jewel* and *jewel* to *juggle*.

But the reader wants "real philosophy." Not this mistery and mixogamy, this phony Symphony in M—for Mystery, Mother, Membrane, Matrix. With maybe some real Mayhem tossed in. Not this wilted "word salad," this logopoeia, this Lyly-gelding, he means, this syllabub of syllables.

Sorry. It's my anima nature to go for the jugglery, baby. (*From afar*: Laughter in the slaughter house.) A burble of purple. Wash your hands of it if you will.

#

So there we are again still, reading and writing, wrighting, unrighting, rewriting, and reeding. Warping away the barbaric woof. A clarinet duet. A net of little clarines, hatching ends with thatching means.

"The end and the means, the gamester and the game,—life is made up of the intermixture and reaction of these two amicable powers, whose marriage appears beforehand monstrous, as each denies and tends to abolish the other. We must reconcile the contradictions as we can, but their discord and their concord introduce wild absurdities into our thinking and speech. No sentence will hold the whole truth, and the only way in which we can be just, is by giving ourselves the lie . . . . All the universe over, there is but one thing, this old Two-Face, creator-creature, mind-matter, right-wrong, of which any proposition may be affirmed or denied."

Emerson, "Nominalist and Realist"

In Schlegel's deathlessly disappearing formulation, "It's equally fatal for the mind to have a system and to have none. It will simply have to decide to combine the two." (Trans. Peter Firchow.)

"Simply," ah, simply.

"Simplify, simplify": thus Thoreau, repeating William of Occam, as well as himself.

O spinster Muses of crossed eyes and dotty teas!

Inde pedem sospes multa cum laude reflexit
errabunda regens tenui vestigial filo,
ne labyrintheis e flexibus egredientem
tecti frustraretur inobservabili error.
                    Catullus, LXIV

And the hero returned in safety, showered with praise,
Guiding his fallible feet with a slender thread.
Missteps unnoticed had otherwise foiled his attempt
To leave the building's winding paths behind.
                    (Trans. David Mulroy)

And then pedate safe pace multiplying laud reflects it
errorabunding regions tenuous thread guiding him feeling
noil labyrinth's haze of flecks high walls a gradient timed
tactile whose forest might turn inobservably his error.
                    (Trans. Louis Zukofsky)

But why digress? James Gleick, on the "poetry" in science, quotes Herman Minkowski: "Space of itself and time of itself will sink into mere shadows, and only a kind of union between them will survive." What kind of union could his one be? Minotauroid? Hippogriffic? Crabapplelike? Or pangolinesque, laurelled and loricate alike.

It is one or another—or their progeny—at the climax of "Notes toward a Supreme Fiction":

> It is possible, possible, possible. It must
> Be possible. It must be that in time
> The real will from its crude compoundings come,
>
> Seeming, at first, a beast disgorged, unlike,
> Warmed by a desperate milk. To find the real,
> To be stripped of every fiction except one,
>
> The fiction of an absolute—Angel,
> Be silent in your luminous cloud and hear
> The luminous melody of proper sound.

"Luminous": not the "voluminous" product of the "master folded in his fire," who is rejected with such grandiloquent scorn in the poem's opening section. "Simplify." But there is a limit: "every fiction" (every fabrication) "except" that of an "absolute" (James Merrill discovered that stringed instrument where the old luthier had buried it). So it is that Nanzia Nunzio parodies this absolute when (fantasizing about Mallarmé) she divests herself before Ozymandias:

> I am the woman stripped more nakedly
> Than nakedness, standing before an inflexible
> Order, saying I am the contemplated spouse.

But Oz, we know from Shelley and the actual toppled gargantuan statue of Ramses II in the Valley of the Kings, has turned out to be frangible in his inflexibility—rigor unmortised, one might say. Nanzia's attempt to mirror in her nakedness the ithyphallic singular itself is doomed—as her soul's imagined spouse, now flexible, lexible, and ultimately altogether exible has learned:

> Then Ozymandias said the spouse, the bride
> Is never naked. A fictive covering
> Weaves always glistening from the heart and mind.

In contradistinction to the alleged "nakedness," there is what Stevens calls (in the first section of "Notes") "Happy fecundity, the flor-abundant force." This florabundance involves both a burgeoning and a flowing, both *flor-* and *fluor-*, and appears (at the end) as "my green, my fluent mundo," also addressed as "Fat girl, terrestrial, my summer, my night." The original "project for the sun" eventuates in a recovery less of Mother Earth than of what she means, which is also the moon, a part of Earth in its beginning and still there in the "mundo" and the "night" and the mutability and the feminine gender.

Stevens also calls his "Fat girl" "the more than natural figure" and "The fiction that results from feeling." He divined what Calvert Watkins has since averred, that "figure" and "fiction" alike derive from the Indo-European *dheigh-*, "to form, to build," which yields the Old English *daege*, "bread-kneader," hence LADY, in addition to *peri-daeza*, "paradise," [a place] walled around by clay kneaded [like dough (by a woman)].

#

Dough: money. No! Yes: the reader's right. No scrip in scraps. Look at this stuff. Riffrough. All over the place. First begging the question then bagging it. Quarrying the query. Crawling out of the wordwork.

How can it keep us from dying, after all, all this—this "doily-making"?

"[Miss Gurley's] house is littered with scraps of cloth and tissue-paper patterns, yellow, pinked, with holes in the shapes of A, B, C, and D in them and numbers; and threads everywhere like a fine vegetation. She has a bosom full of needles with threads ready to pull out and make nests with. She sleeps in her thimble. A gray kitten once lay on the treadle of her sewing machine, where she rocked it as she sewed, like a baby in a cradle, but it got hanged on the belt. Or did she make that up? But another gray-and-white one lies now by the arm of the machine, in imminent danger of being sewn into a turban. There is a table covered with laces and braids, embroidery silks, and cards of buttons of all colors—big ones for winter coats, small pearls, little glass delicious ones to suck."

Bishop, "In the Village"

After writing her first drafts of "One Art," Bishop set down a potential rhyme scheme: "ABA ABA." Then came the idea of the villanelle, a pattern that had been there on the poet's sewing table for who knows how long. How many of her earlier subjects had been mangled in composition? The little glass buttons "delicious to suck" repeat the five-cent piece the child swallows. Do both glass buttons and coin stand in, fill in, like words, for tender buttons of the absent mother?

"The inner, subtle essences can be contemplated only by sucking, not by knowing."

Isaac the Blind (12th–13th century), quoted in
Daniel C. Matt, *The Essential Kabbalah*

At the end of "Filling Station" Bishop speculates that "somebody / arranges the rows" of oil cans "so that they softly say: / ESSO—SO—SO / To high-strung automobiles." "Somebody." The missing mother, who has embroidered the doily on the filling station's "grease- / impregnated" taboret? Or the now absconded poet, who still sees (and insists by virtue of her line break after "grease-" that we see) how the "doily" soaks up "oily"? Or is there a difference? Sew—sew—sew.

"Two pale, smooth wooden hoops are pressed together in the linen. There is a case of little ivory embroidery tools.

"I abscond with a little ivory stick with a sharp point. To keep it forever I bury it under the bleeding heart by the crab-apple tree, but it is never found again."

Bishop, "In the Village"

#

"Crab-apple": what a term. For my reader. But "the identity of the word—the simple, fundamental fact of language, that there are fewer terms of designation than there are things to designate—is itself a two-sided experience: it reveals words as the unexpected meeting place of the most distant figures of reality . . . . In their wealth of poverty words always refer away from and lead back to themselves; they are lost and found again and again . . . . The mystified guests [in Raymond Roussel's *Impressions d'Afrique*] must have realized this while going around the billiard table, when they discovered that the straight line of words was identical to their circular path."

Michel Foucault, *Death and the Labyrinth* (trans. Charles Ruas)

One thinks of Djuna Barnes's twining and twinning of "bridal" and "bridle" paths in mazy *Nightwood* and of how generative that coincidence was. It overlaps with her equally unlikely doubling of "race" (a dubious subgroup of humanity) and "race" (a competition). Then there is her "leg" motif—it takes "legs" to run and runners to run "legs" of races—which in turn gets tangled up with those of the legless, including the lugubrious Mademoiselle Basquette, and the legendary, like Nikka, who, nearly as naked as Nanzia, "used to fight the bear in the Cirque de Paris":

"'There he was, crouching all over the arena without a stitch on, except an ill-concealed loin-cloth . . . tattooed from head to heel with all the ameublement of depravity! Garlanded with rosebuds and hackwork of the devil—was he a sight to see! Though he couldn't have done a thing . . . if you had stood him in a gig-mill for a week, though (it's said) at a stretch it spelled Desdemona. Well then, over his belly was an angel from Chartres: on each buttock, half public, half private, a quotation from the Jansenist theory . . . . Across his knees, I give you my word, "I" on one and on the other "can," put those together! Across his chest, beneath a beautiful caravel in full sail, two clasped hands, the wrist bones fretted with point lace. On each bosom an arrow-speared heart, each with different initials but with equal drops of blood.'"

The heart's needle and the bleeding heart, the distaff and the spear.

In the packing company, on the kill room floor, among the offal—soggy rugs of honeycombed tripe, barrels of bittersweet peachy cheeks, hooves and tails, gullets, spongy lights, and fluky livers—the blood coagulated in the tubs in archipelagoes, cells seeking still to clot and stanch the flow.

"'And the legs?' Felix asked uncomfortably.
"'The legs,' said Doctor O'Connor, 'were devoted entirely to vine work, topped by the swart rambler rose . . . . I asked him why all this barbarity; he answered he loved beauty and would have it about him.'"

If Nikka caricatures Othello, the tragically dimidiate figure—and epitomizes the black whole of the novel *Nightwood* (itself a farrago of splendid and scabrous things, piracy and poetry, Black Mass and mysticism)—he also conjures Cain. Since what you get—after you have got "Can I"—when you put together the "I" and the "can" on his knees is the brother of Abel—who is but cannot be his brother's keeper. Which is to say "I can" is "Cain" who should be able. Yet Nikka who is Cain is exactly not Abel. So whether he is and is not Othello, an Inca himself, he is the race. Hence, lost.

"Another lost book is good old *Nightwood* . . . . *Nightwood* would also be good for someone here who likes purple prose."
                              Bishop, letter to May Swenson

"Lost" but in her blood. And purple as the rambler rose. As the bleeding heart. Isn't it the "sharp point" that the lost needle gives rise to the shrub's flowers? That *to sew* is *to sow*?

But that's not a point, you might say. But maybe there is no point, Grim Reader. My onlie Reaper. *Mon frère*. Brothers, weepers; losers, keepers. It's all strings some think now, thank you. Strings making chords. Language's necklace's a lucky synecdoche. (Though for aught we ought know we know aught.) Or call it all Auld Lang's Lay. Every stitch and stich, stick, stock, and stone of it. Weigh it all out. Whatever we pay and play and pray up and on in this whole mind-mined, must-moiled, logo-rolling, ball-bearing multiverse.

VI

Blue Guide

I'd like to retire there and do nothing . . .

—ELIZABETH BISHOP (1911–1979)

On this small island that undoes us daily, gently,
It's hard to take too seriously, too intently
A town whose name means *town*
(As well as *country*, *land*, and *nation*—
Exemplary synecdoche, one notes, even on vacation),
And which has just two buses
(One labors to and from the gritty port,
The other wheezes to and from the smaller, higher town),
Each of which, when seen,
As usually, from a hill, inching up a slope or down,
Appears a cross between a donkey and a wind-up toy.
In cans, no less, the ferry brings in gasoline . . .
(It's hard, too, not to think of *you* in such outskirts.)
The gates to miniature courtyards
Before the two-room houses are just two feet high.
The bent and agèd widow in black crêpe,
Her groceries at her hip (as no doubt in her heart a sigh),
Must stoop to open hers.

The one bus driver, who guides his glossy, truly verdigris
Mercedes from this main town to the country,
Is a kind of hero, according to Sabine
(Whose name rhymes with the French noun *cabinet*,
All that she—German, verb, wild, and self-exiled—seems not to be).
He has no room for error
On his steep way, so ever narrower

It is as though his wheels ran on a track.
They *should be* on a track.
There are few children of school age here,
And so on any given bus ride the fates of many
Are in his hands, both on the wheel.
From his one rear-view mirror dangles
A silken, tangle-tasseled noose of amber worry beads,
A pale and bruised (or smudged) St. Christopher,
An "eye," or *máti*, as they say in Greek—
Even more circumspectly apotropaic,
With its three ovals of white paint
Around the oval smalt glass bead recalling the Graeae.
Into an indentation in his dash
(Where a clock would go, if there were time)
Someone has pasted Jesus as a sugary shepherd.
In tourist season he'll pack thirty souls
Into this vehicle whose capacity, so its doors state,
Is fourteen. Now and then, the van must stop, must wait
For a herd of goats or a straggle of donkeys and *their* driver
To let it have the oxbow in the road.

When he is at the helm he does not smoke,
Though lounging in the shady square in Chóra
(*Chóra . . . chóra . . .* in the *Timaeus* womb and home
Of everything that moves and changes form),
Where he seems so out of his element, alert
And nervy as a sailor after his long voyage,
Ears plugged with last year's Walkman,
He works his beads through like a penitent and smokes,
Smokes like a fuse . . . But he never jokes,
And one cannot imagine him, unlike the town's
Other several Kostases (Kostádes?),
Sipping an endless watered ouzo,

Of an evening, whose sweet cloudiness,
The product of opposing clarities,
He can't afford the licorice vestiges of—
The lickerish, languid, lackadaisical effects of.
So when Iríni, lost in her twelve-year-old fog of love,
Doesn't disembark, he knows—and calls her forth.
He has black, curly hair, thick as with suint, a thick moustache.
Vigilant, he wears dark, dark sunglasses with thin gold rims
Against the vigilant sun.

The other driver—like his van's springs—is bouncier.
Stars glitter in his dark brown eyes.
He has a smile that shows off one gold eyetooth.
He has his amulets as well: a gilt cross,
A pair of fuzzy dice (elephantoid), a string of olive beads,
And then—isn't it?—a garlic bulb, ceramic.
His bus is two-tone: jaded yellow over faded brown.
He drives toward sunrise, as Kóstas toward sunset.
And back, of course. They both drive back,
Each to his end of the town.

One never sees the two together.
But they are brothers—maybe twins, but unmistakably they're brothers—
Even here where everyone's related.
Unless there are not really two of them.
So could there be one brother, as it were, in different modes?
If there are two, the one who flashes glinting smiles
And has a three-note horn he blows on his arrival
Has neatly lettered advertisements in his bus:
"Hotel Odysseas," "Atlantides Souvenirs," "Caïque from Yannis"
(Calligraphy in the same hand).
There are no solicitations in the other bus,
There being no place visitors would want to stay, so many miles

From any shop, though there are still some residents
In the high village, its dwellings clinging to the road.
(For centuries the governments have made it the abode
Of favorite scapegoat dissidents.
It's one thing that this unknown place is known for.
One thing I think of *your* approving in it,
This isle that's still an exile,
Come to seem the perfect home
For certain types, who wouldn't—couldn't—change,
And yet who *needed* change, demanded *change* . . .)
Dimítrios makes change. Dispenses tickets—
After the ride, in careful trade for fare—
As though his ride alone were not worth 13 cents.

Our dourer driver does not deal out useless stubs.
He will provide directions,
Since there are several paths that lead off from his terminus.
There is the path to Déndro, or Tree, where on some days
On the horizon islands ride at anchor in a lavender haze
(Itself a product of opposing clarities),
And other days in the penumbra of the sky and sea
The only island that an eye can see
Is the idea of an island, forming for the very gaze,
Rather like *idea* in the Attic verb *to see*,
Precipitating itself, viewed as through gauze,
As vague as *its* Greek source through *tiffany*.

Another path leads to Angáli, and then, beyond some rocks,
There's a sliver of a beach where, on any given day,
The hiker might find Sabine.
A sort of tutelary spirit, ageless,
Although by now pure body, like a fish,
She eats the island's bread and bitter olives,

Drinks its *ráki*, knows its coverts for the night,
And walks barefoot as though in boots
Through donkey dung and loose sharp rock.
Suddenly she stood,
In surfsuds washing ankle bracelets,
Browned all over, blonde hair bleached wheat and white,
Facing the sun, hands piling her hair up—
And when she turned, a tuft of shining copper filaments.

There is the path to Zodóchos Pýgi, the Church of the Fountain of Life,
A chastened venue, blued, sparely furnished—
No blind mouths here—
Although the name, when said aloud,
Calls up an animal, a stuffed or stuffy cartoon character.
There has to be as well a path to that white chapel,
Distant, guarded on one side
By what must be the island's only six Italian cypresses.
It looks like *the* local example, oddly estranged,
Of architecture ecclesiastical.
But then when one can't find it on the map at all,
It seems it was a crisp mirage.

Some paths fray out in scrub and friable hardscrabble.
Life is tough, says the thistle—and the furze says so too.
Life is tough, the stone groans back, as the plants squeeze through.

And there's the broad path to the Church of Pandelídhis,
Cobbled with stones the shades of almonds and pistachios.
As smooth by now as used soap bars,
As sucked-on lozenges, and sweetly modulated,
They make the spirit's dry mouth water for watercolors.
The church itself's a painful white in sun,
And in the wind the courtyard's two bay laurels

Make their gull-like noises,
And dry leaves scramble crablike back and forth
Across the ancient stones outlined last month with luscious white.

The wind gusts up there, scented with sage, or thyme,
And blows away like gossip on the square.

Zigzagging up from Chóra there's the path to the Panaghía,
The Church of the Madonna, perched above all else,
In daylight irresistible as a Carème meringue,
Within whose shadow for a moment one might think—
So this is where I've always meant to be:
Near these eroding ruins of a Venetian aerie,
At cliff's edge, just above where someone, not long ago,
Risking a neck to do it, built a little course of stones,
And set an orange crate in it.
And this is where I want to stay (so one might think),
Spying, or *overseeing*, really, *speculating*,
And *skeptical* if need be, and meanwhile
Painting, drafting, drifting off in misty blue,
Doing the nothing special,
The special nothing one was born and bred to do.
Surrounded by outcroppings splashed with lichen,
Orange, pinkish, gray, and charcoal
(Or thriving, aging, dying, dead),
Among the goat turds like large coffee beans,
Letting the wind whip through *Geography III*
(Since I'd nothing if not time),
I'd watch the azure sea
Turn up like plowed-down sillions in white water,
Muse on the mazy alleys down in town,
Follow a thought beyond that shotgun blast of bougainvillea,
Sudden, unanswerable as a ruptured aneurysm,

Beyond the very corner first
Turned—when? thirty years ago by now?—
That juncture where I slipped somehow
Into this iridescent bubble of the future
Waiting itself to burst . . .

And I would know how in that notebook
Were seeds of all the verse I'd ever want to make,
The poems it would take forever to have made,
Not one day more or less,
Poems modeled on the Wandering Islands,
A constellation of them, like the Kykládes, but in motion,
An archipelago loosely kaleidoscopic
Called sometimes "Neighborhood of a Point,"
Sometimes—less mathematically—"Klitórides," or "Little Hills" . . .

How slow the evening is down there, beneath the Panaghía,
Where by now the chickens turn on their rotisseries,
*Pop*ping, *pop*ping—like the men out shooting *trigoniá*;
Where, later, deep in his taverna, Níkos clears up mysteries
(*Ah, naí, tó nekrotapheío*—the cemetery);
Where next door to my house a single workman paves
A courtyard with the sea stone that's a kind of glaucous slate,
The Aegean's color on a cloudy day (with ingrained waves).
One family specializes in the cutting of it in the north
And in the southern shaping of it into those thin plates.
How quiet everything is here,
Quite as quiet the deepened light.
If you could scoop a little of it up—the light, the quiet—
The lucid color of a pristine sapphire
Like water in your hands . . .
But then, always before you're ready for it,
It's dark. It is dark . . .

Though if you stay there long enough you might meet Sabine.
If you do, maybe she'll go with you,
As the stucco glows brighter and colder,
Through the gates, and show you how to climb the church,
And where to lie down on the dome
(By now the whitewash is like sculpted snow,
Her burnished tones, by moonlight, a moontan),
And pick out patterns that the stars prick out.
What happens next is always pure improvisation.

Before departing, take the green bus out to its last stop,
Where Kóstas can point out an extravagant path
That finally reaches the island's tip,
Ambéli, or Vineyard,
Paradise at our world's end,
With tiny gardens lifted from the *Georgics*—
Gardens quite distinct (like the Islands of the Blessèd
In the Age of Gold, when *death* meant sleep as rich as honey,
When *food* meant honey, fruit, and vegetables),
Gardens of persimmon, quince, edged with shady olive trees
(The olive trees unpaintable, indeed, unprintable,
Barely moving in the barest breeze
As though a rain were falling silkily—
Although it's not: see, there are Virgil's bees),
Grape vines, melons, sweet corn, while bamboo sweeps the sky,
Sweet water runs on the surface, small frogs jump,
And (I swear) cows graze—
And one crow always sits on one cow's rump
(Unless the cows take turns).
And from the beach (since here there's always time)
You must swim to the caverns,
As "quickly cold as death," to cadge from Sabine,
Who takes you in to where,

As in some mad Cyclopic ear, black water gurgles,
Sloshes, slaps, and echoes, re-echoes . . .

But it's a matchless brilliant of a bay
You gasp back out to see
(From the beach no bigger than a minute,
As someone in the family used to say),
Wherein the water's beryl green,
The blues our small Earth is from lunar vantage, marine
Mixed with milori, maybe, or blue turquoise—or is it
Berlin blue? Or Brunswick blue?
Or since from my own point of view
The changing hue is so somehow suffused with you,
Bishop blue, episcopal—is flat exquisite.